Pebble®

Our Community Helpers

Dentists Help

by Dee Ready

Consulting editor: Gail Saunders-Smith, PhD

CAPSTONE PRESS
a capstone imprint

Pebble Books are published by Capstone Press,
1710 Roe Crest Drive, North Mankato, Minnesota 56003
www.capstonepub.com

Library of Congress Cataloging-in-Publication Data
Cataloging-in-Publication information is on file with the Library of Congress.
ISBN: 978-1-62065-081-3 (library binding)
ISBN: 978-1-62065-841-3 (paperback)
ISBN: 978-1-4765-1714-8 (ebook PDF)

Note to Parents and Teachers

The Our Community Helpers set supports national social studies
standards for how groups and institutions work to meet individual
needs. This book describes and illustrates dentists. The images
support early readers in understanding the text. The repetition of
words and phrases helps early readers learn new words. This book
also introduces early readers to subject-specific vocabulary words,
which are defined in the Glossary section. Early readers may need
assistance to read some words and to use the Table of Contents,
Glossary, Read More, Internet Sites, and Index sections of the book.

Table of Contents

What Is a Dentist?

Dentists help people
care for their teeth.
Dentists fix teeth.
They also help people
keep their teeth healthy.

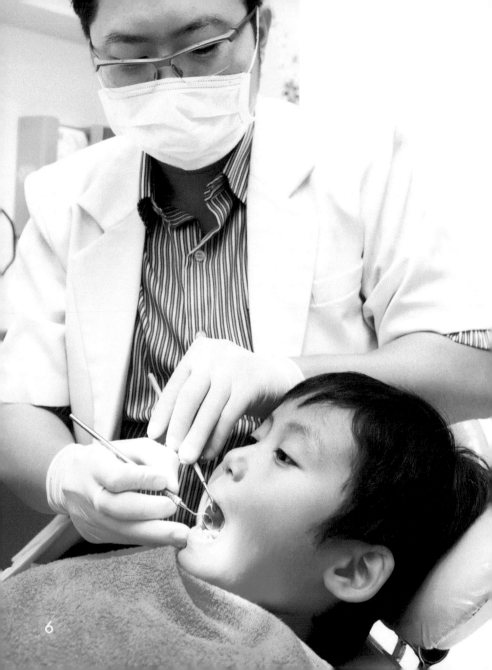

Some dentists do special jobs.
Some fix only children's teeth.
They are called pediatric
dentists. Orthodontists fix
crooked teeth.

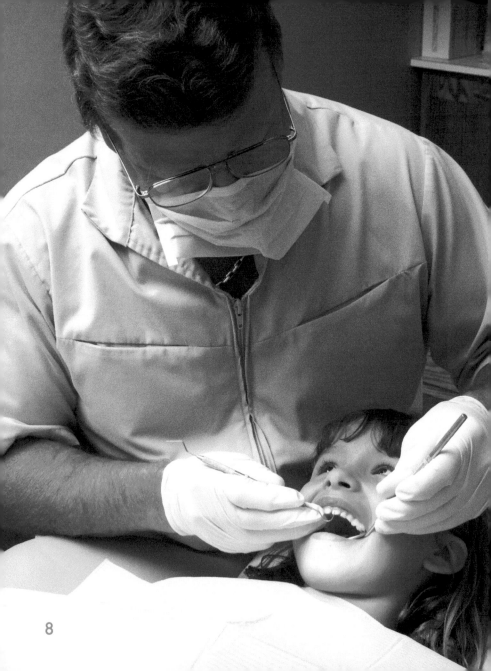

What Dentists Do

People go to dentists
for checkups. Dentists check
teeth for cavities.
They also check to see
if gums are healthy.

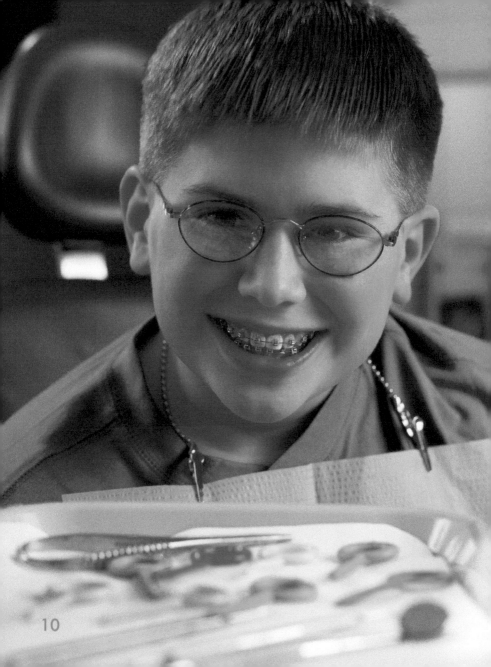

Dentists fix problems
they find. They fill cavities.
Orthodontists might put
braces on crooked teeth.

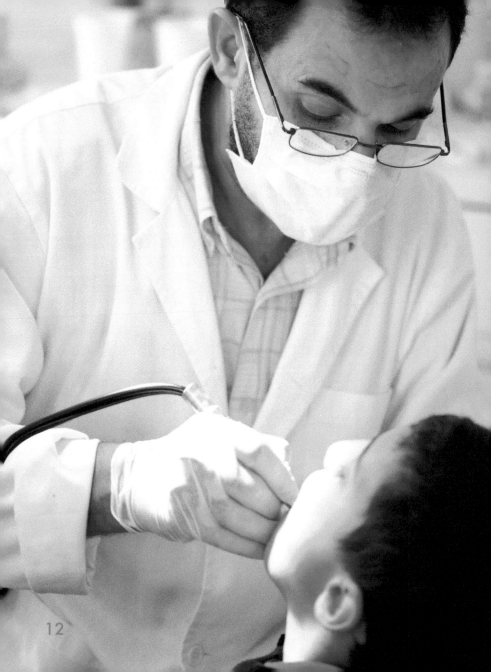

Clothes and Tools

Dentists may wear white coats to see patients. They may also wear scrubs. Rubber gloves and masks protect dentists and patients from germs.

x-ray

Dentists gather information with tools. Small mirrors help them see in the mouth. X-rays help them see cavities.

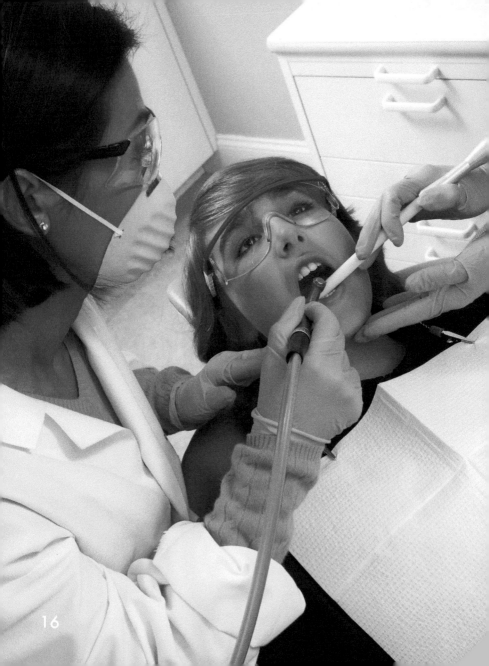

Dentists have tools to fix teeth.
They use drills to fix cavities.
They use tools to suck up
extra spit when working
in the mouth.

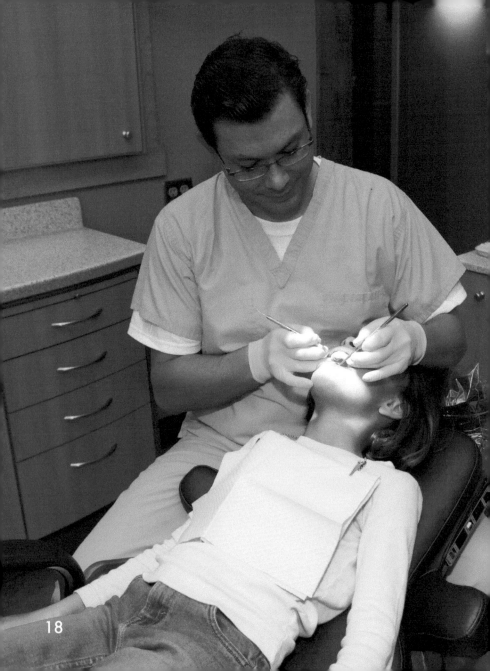

Where Dentists Work

Most dentists work in their own offices. Other dentists work in clinics. All dentists have exam rooms with dental chairs so patients can lie back.

Dentists Help

Dentists help people in the community care for their teeth. A dentist's work gives people strong, healthy teeth for life.

Glossary

braces—a device attached to teeth to pull them into position and make them straight

cavity—a hole in a tooth caused by decay

checkup—an exam to see if a person is healthy

clinic—a building where people or animals go to get medical care

germ—a very tiny living thing that can cause disease

gum—the firm flesh around the base of a person's tooth

healthy—fit and well, not sick

patient—a person who gets medical care

scrubs—a loose, lightweight uniform worn by workers in clinics and hospitals

x-ray—a picture taken of the inside of the body that can show if something is wrong

Read More

Gorman, Jacqueline Laks. *Dentists.* People in My Community. New York: Gareth Stevens Pub., 2011.

Guillain, Charlotte. *Visiting the Dentist.* Growing Up. Chicago: Heinemann Library, 2011.

Salzmann, Mary Elizabeth. *Dentist's Tools.* Professional Tools. Minneapolis: ABDO Pub., 2011.

Internet Sites

FactHound offers a safe, fun way to find Internet sites related to this book. All of the sites on FactHound have been researched by our staff.

Here's all you do:

Visit *www.facthound.com*

Type in this code: 9781620650813

Super-cool stuff! Check out projects, games and lots more at **www.capstonekids.com**

23

Index

Word Count: 183
Grade: 1
Early-Intervention Level: 19

Editorial Credits
Gillia Olson, editor; Gene Bentdahl, designer; Eric Manske, production specialist

Photo Credits
Capstone Studio: Karon Dubke, cover, 8, 18; Corbis RF, 4, 10, 14, 20; Shutterstock: bikeriderlondon, 16, Realinemedia, 6, ZouZou, 12